ISBN 978-0-265-00312-1
PIBN 10964179

1 MONTH OF
FREE
READING

at
www.ForgottenBooks.com

By purchasing this book you are eligible for one month membership to ForgottenBooks.com, giving you unlimited access to our entire collection of over 1,000,000 titles via our web site and mobile apps.

To claim your free month visit:
www.forgottenbooks.com/free964179

English
Français
Deutsche
Italiano
Español
Português

www.forgottenbooks.com

Mythology Photography **Fiction**
Fishing Christianity **Art** Cooking
Essays Buddhism Freemasonry
Medicine **Biology** Music **Ancient
Egypt** Evolution Carpentry Physics
Dance Geology **Mathematics** Fitness
Shakespeare **Folklore** Yoga Marketing
Confidence Immortality Biographies
Poetry **Psychology** Witchcraft
Electronics Chemistry History **Law**
Accounting **Philosophy** Anthropology
Alchemy Drama Quantum Mechanics
Atheism Sexual Health **Ancient History**
Entrepreneurship Languages Sport
Paleontology Needlework Islam
Metaphysics Investment Archaeology
Parenting Statistics Criminology
Motivational

VOL. 7.   SEPTEMBER 5, 1923.   NO. 10.

CROP PROSPECTS.

Forecast Hungarian Production 1923 larger than 1922 for corn, potatoes, and sugar beets. Forecasts of corn production in Hungary, 1923, is 53,186,000 bushels as compared with 32,493,000 bushels in 1922, according to a cablegram to the United States Department of Agriculture from the International Institute of Agriculture at Rome. This is an increase of 20,693,000 bushels over the production of last year.

The potato production is forecasted at 65,439,000 bushels against 33,859,000 in 1922.

Forecasts of sugar beet production indicate a crop of 974,000 short tons as compared with 632,000 short tons produced last year.

Increase in Egyptian Cotton crop. Egyptian cotton production for 1923 is forecasted at 1,204,000 bales (478 pounds net) as compared with 1,015,000 bales for last year, according to a cable received by the United States Department of Agriculture on August 29, from the International Institute of Agriculture in Rome. This preliminary forecast indicates an increase of 18.6 per cent over the final estimate for last year.

Bavaria's grain crops increased. 1923 German bread grain acreage increased. Sugar beet area increased. Potatoes same as last year. Reports indicate that the area of wheat to be harvested in Germany this year is about 10 per cent less than last year, but the area of rye is 10 per cent greater, making the total area of bread grains to be harvested greater than last year. The area in potatoes appears to be about the same as last year. The sugar beet area has been considerably increased. The total acreage for Germany in 1922 was 3,396,000 acres for wheat; 10,236,000 acres for rye, 6,725,000 acres for potatoes, and 1,031,000 acres for sugar beets.

Bavaria's wheat crop is forecasted at 14,918,000 bushels compared to 11,213,000, an increase of 3,705,000 or 33.0 per cent. The rye crop is forecasted at 21,849,000 bushels against 20,537,000, an increase of 1,312,000 bushels or 6.4 per cent. The production of barley is forecasted at 24,434,000 bushels compared with 17,337,000 bushels last year. The increase amounts to 7,097,000 bushels. Oats production is forecasted at 41,819,000 bushels compared with 28,992,000 bushels in 1922. This means an increase of 12,827,000 bushels more than last year. The spelt crop this year is forecasted at 1,543,000 bushels against 1,259,000 bushels last year, an increase of 284,000 bushels.

Bavaria in 1922 had 19.8 per cent of the total wheat acreage of Germany; 10.6 per cent of the total rye acreage; 26.0 per cent of the summer barley acreage; 13.1 per cent of oats; and 17.0 per cent of winter spelt.

Crop conditions in Norway improved during August, but are still below
the September 1 condition last year, according to a radiogram received September 1 by the United States Department of Agriculture from the Department
of Agriculture at Kristiania. The condition of the wheat crop on September
1 was 86 per cent of the ten-year average compared with 83 per cent last
month and 94 per cent on September 1 last year. Rye was 98 per cent compared with 97 per cent last month and 101 last year. The condition of oats
was 75 compared with 74 last month and 92 last year. Barley was 80 compared
with 76 last month and 98 last year. The condition of potatoes was 89 compared with 85 last month and 102 last year.

Increased acreage in Argentina for wheat, oats and Linseed. According
to a radiogram received by the United States Department of Agriculture on
September 2, 1923, from the International Institute of Agriculture at Rome,
the area sown to wheat in Argentina is estimated for the 1923-24 season to be
17,038,000 acres as compared with 15,940,000 acres for the 1922-23 season,
an increase of 7 per cent. The oats area is estimated at 2,632,000 acres as
compared to 2,618,000 acres. The flax area for 1923-24 is estimated to be
4,824,000 acres compared to 4,112,000 acres for 1922-23.

Argentine live stock census. The Argentine Embassy reports that the
1922 Livestock Census shows the number of cattle in Argentina to be 37,064,150
compared with 25,866,763 given in the 1914 census, and the 1919 estimate of
27,720,832. This indicates an increase of 43.3 per cent over the 1914 census
and 33.7 per cent over the 1919 estimate. The sheep in 1922 numbered 35,671,000
compared with 43,225,452 given in the 1914 census. This shows a reduction of
7,554,452 sheep in 1922 or a decrease of 17.5 per cent over the 1914 census
figures. During the first eight months of 1923, the slaughterings of cattle
increased 40 per cent over the slaughterings last year. The report states
that these figures are subject to verification.

GERMAN FAT AND OIL SITUATION.

Revolutionary changes in the German fat and oil industry during and
since the war may have an important bearing upon the future profitableness of
several products of American agriculture.

There has been a considerable reduction in supplies of fats in Germany
since the beginning of the war. No data are available to show how low the
supplies fell during the war. There have been some improvements in supplies
since the war but they are still low. The best available data indicate that
the total supply for 1922 was only 70 per cent of the total supply for 1912-13.
The reduction of the population from 68,000,000 in 1912-13 to 60,000,600 in
1922 reduces the need for fats but the per capita supply is only 80 per cent
of the prewar supply.

Germany produces a smaller proportion of her total fat supplies than
she produced before the war. In 1912-13 fifty-eight per cent of the German
fats and oils were home produced from domestic animals, home-grown seeds and
imported seeds and all other materials from which the fats had not been ex-
tracted. In 1922 home production constituted only 49 per cent of the total
supply.

GERMAN FAT AND OIL SITUATION, CONT'D.

Probably the most significant change since the beginning of the war is the tendency to replace animal fats, pork fats in particular, with other and cheaper fats, chiefly from vegetables. The relative position of pork fats has declined from 33 per cent of the total in 1912-13 to 24 per cent in 1922. The per capita use of pork fats has decreased about 42 per cent, whereas the use of all fats and oils has decreased only about 20 per cent.

Germany was an important exporter of vegetable oils in pre-war years, but in 1922 was obliged to import large quantities. Net exports averaged 39,300 tons for the years 1912 and 1913, while net imports amounted to 147,858 tons in 1922. Post-war oil production from imported materials, although increasing, is still below that of pre-war years.

Copra was the most important oil-containing raw material imported into Germany in 1922, and was the only material to exceed pre-war tonnage. Palm kernels and rape and rapeseed were next in importance.

German imports of margarine materials in 1922, with the exception of fish oil, were below pre-war figures, although margarine production is estimated to have been twice what it was before the war. The deficiency has been filled by vegetable oils which are used for other purposes as well.

The fall in imports of these materials has been largely at the expense of the United States.

Fat supplies from slaughtered cattle, based upon dressed weights, with 1922 considered as 100, was as follows in the years indicated: 1921, 90; 1920, 50; 1919, 62; and 1913, 147. Fat supplies from hogs slaughtered in 1922 were from 40 to 45 per cent of the 1912-13 total.

The number of dairy cattle in Germany in 1922 was 80 per cent of the pre-war figure. Milk goats, of which there are a large number, increased 30 per cent during the same period.

Trade in dairy products, both imports and exports, with the exception of cheese, is much below that of pre-war years.

Germany (Occupied Territory), in virtue of a Decision issued from Coblenz on July 13, according to the Board of Trade Journal and Commercial Gazette, July 26, 1923, oilcakes (residues from the manufacture of fatty oils) may be exported from the Occupied Territory without payment of export duty, and without requirement of export license. In addition, these oilcakes may be exported from Occupied to Unoccupied Germany without permit formality.

GERMAN FAT AND OIL SITUATION,-CONT'D.

Pork supplies in Germany will be somewhat larger next winter than they were last year owing to a considerable increase in the number of hogs in Prussia. The hog census of Prussia June 30, bears out the forecast made by the Department in May, of an increase in the number of hogs in Germany. The number for the whole of Prussia was estimated to be nearly 10 per cent greater than at the same time last year. An analysis of the figures for the two years shows that there has been nearly 25 per cent increase in the number of spring pigs and 16 per cent increase in the number of brood sows. It is estimated that home production will meet about two-thirds of the domestic requirements. The increase may be expected to diminish somewhat the demand for American pork and lard in the coming year. However, the number of hogs in the country is far below pre-war normal, and the demand for foreign meats and fats will continue large.

Census of June 1st	1923	1922
Pig holding Households	2,819,549	2,756,770
Farrows of less than 8 weeks	2,244,545	1,804,947
Young pigs of less than 6 months	4,638,165	4,514,676
Boars of less than one year	31,045	26,793
Brood sows of less than 1 year	418,937	339,989
All other pigs " " " "	1,133,093	1,276,396
Boars of 1 year and more	28,020	26,761
Brood Sows of one year and older	625,013	560,383
All other pigs of one year and older	141,902	133,991
Grand Total	9,460,720	8,683,936

Owing to the occupation of the Ruhr District, the totals given are probably less than the actual number of hogs because of the difficulties experienced in getting figures.

GERMAN OIL TRADE. 1912, 1913, - 1922.

Year	Oil Imports.	Oil Exports.	Import Surplus.	Export Surplus.	Oil from Seeds Imported	Total available for consumption
	Short tons	Short tons	Short tons	Short tons	Short tons	Short tons
1912 ..	106,741	126,201	......	19,460	582,689	563,229
1913 ..	88,165	147,304	......	59,139	703,797	644,658
1912/13:						
average:	97,453	136,752	......	39,300	693,243	603,943
1922 ..	166,853	18,995	147,858	......	414,243	562,101

PRODUCTION OF WHEAT, ALL COUNTRIES REPORTING, 1922 AND 1923.

	Production.		Per Cent of 1922.	
	1922.	1923.	Decrease	Increase
	Bushels	Bushels	Per Cent	Per Cent
Estimates previously received and unrevised, 22 countries	2,323,194,000	2,415,765,000		4.0
Estimates recently received	None	None		

Source: Official sources and International Institute of Agriculture.

Exports of Grains and Wheat Flour from the United States, Wheat and Wheat
Flour from Canada, and Shipments of Canadian Wheat and Wheat Flour
through the United States in transit, July and August 1922
and 1923, and August 11 to September 1, 1923.

Commodity	Unit	July and August		1923		
		1922	1923 Prelim- inary.	Week ending August 18	Week ending Aug.25.	Week ending Sept.1.
		1,000	1,000	1,000	1,000	1,000
Exports:						
Barley	Bu.	4,604	4,237	383	932	289
Corn	"	26,414	1,760	220	126	100
Oats	"	5,944	420	12	22	99
Rye	"	7,399	4,476	248	79	501
Wheat	"	48,682	32,143	3,901	3,271	8,215
Wheat Flour	Bbls.	2,090	1,831	233	276	264
In transit shipments from Canada:						
Wheat	Bu.	7,675	7,118	203	362	205
Wheat Flour	Bbls.	298	247	1	2	1
Exports from Canada:		July	July			
Wheat	Bu.	9,487	12,665			
Wheat Flour	Bbls.	486	775			

Source: U. S. Department of Commerce and Monthly Reports of the Trade of Canada.

COTTON AREA AND PRODUCTION FORECASTS FOR UNITED STATES, INDIA, AND EGYPT
FOR 1923-24 COMPARED WITH ESTIMATES FOR 1922-23.

Country.	Acreage		Production	
	1922-23	1923-24	1922-23	1923-24
	Acres	Acres	Bales 478 lbs. net	Bales 478 lbs. net
United States ...:	34,016,000:	38,287,000 :	9,762,000 :	10,788,000
India (58% crop).:	a 12,496,000:	a 12,373,000 :	.... :	....
Egypt ....:	1,869,000:	1,516,000 :	1,015,000 :	1,204,000

a First Government forecasts which relate to areas sown up to the end of
July and covers on an average about 58 per cent of the total cotton
area for India. Last year's final estimate was 21,154,000 acres.

COTTON SOWINGS IN RUSSIA.

Cotton sowings in various areas of the Russian Union, according to
the Manchester Guardian of August 2 are: Turkestan 405,000 acres, Caucasus
67,000 acres, Khiva 27,000 acres and Bokhara 27,000 acres. It is stated
that if capital can be found to pay for the crop it is expected that the
area sown will be doubled next year. Announcement has been made that the
Russian Government is giving a credit of six million gold roubles for irri-
gation work in Turkestan.

COTTON CROP PROSPECTS IN MEXICO.

The weather during July was favorable for the development of the
cotton crop in Lower California, according to a report from Consul H. C.
von Struve, Mexicali, Mexico, dated July 30. The heat was constant but
not so great as to injure the crop. It is estimated by some people that
the outlook is for a crop around 90,000 bales, but more conservative ob-
servers, in the light of last year's experience, do not look for a crop
of more than 75,000 bales.

COMPARATIVE TABLE OF THE MOST IMPORTANT GERMAN FAT SUPPLIES.

	1912-13	1922
	Short tons	Short tons
German Production		
Animal Fats		
Hog fat	595,000	265,000
Butter	441,000	292,000
Beef fat	187,000	127,000
Rendering fats (from refuse, bones, etc.) a:	17,000	17,000
Total animal fats	1,240,000	701,000
Vegetable Fats		
Oil from German seeds .	33,000	44,000
Total German production	1,273,000	745,000
Imported Supplies		
Animal Fats		
Hog Fat:		
Lard	118,000	72,000
Fat from fresh pork.	7,000	2,750
Fat from bacon	1,600	22,600
Total Hog Fat ...	126,600	97,350
Butter	61,000	1,180
Butter from imported cream	15,400	......
Premier Jus and Oleo b	50,000	22,000
Tallow and bone fat b	21,000	40,000
Total Animal Fats	274,000	160,530
Fish Oil and Fat b ...	53,000	69,000
Vegetable Fats		
Oil and oil from raw materials b	595,000	551,000
Total Imported Supplies	922,000	730,530
Total all supplies	2,195,000	1,525,530

a - inedible.   b - minus exports.

IMPORTS OF THE MOST IMPORTANT OILS INTO GERMANY.

Item	1912	1913	1922
	Short tons	Short tons	Short tons
Linseed oil	2,963	3,489	32,229
Soya bean oil	12,211	3,461	45,718
Cotton seed oil ...	29,624	17,943	2,935
Castor oil	9,463	10,501	3,868
Palm oil	13,088	16,613	5,627
Palm-kernel oil ...	6	53	4,038
Coconut oil	367	655	32,162
Olein	12,648	13,371	2,162
Total	80,370	66,086	128,739

Source: Report from U.S. Agricultural Representative in Berlin, Germany.

IMPORTS OF THE MOST IMPORTANT OIL SEEDS INTO GERMANY.

Seed	1913	1920	1921	1922
	Short tons	Short tons	Short tons	Short tons
Rape and rape-seed	169,122	9,776	44,887	135,979
Peanuts	108,119	1,097	29,313	76,381
Sesamum	127,909	2,755	38,671	17,281
Linseed and linmeal	617,645	5,849	35,367	113,708
Cottonseed	242,282	58	569	21,399
Soyabeans and				95,246
movra seeds, etc..	138,614	2,509	12,697	8,934
Palm kernel........	260,051	3,002	19,977	139,860
Copra	216,546	10,680	78,110	311,595
Total	1,880,288	35,726	259,591	920,383

Source: U.S. Agricultural Representative in Berlin, Germany.

POSSIBLE GERMAN OIL CAKE PRODUCTION.

Pre-War and Post-War

	Tons of 2,000 Pounds	
Pre-war		
Oil seeds crushed in 1912..........:	1,570,288	
Estimated oil yield 1912............:	582,689	
Possible cake yield................:	987,599	
Oil seeds crushed in 1913...........:	1,911,029	
Estimated oil yield 1913............:	703,797	
Possible cake yield ....:	1,207,232	
Average possible cake yield 1912-13 :		1,097,415
Post-war		
Oil seeds crushed in 1922 ....:	895,972	
Estimated oil yield 1922 ....:	414,244	
Possible cake yield in 1922 ....:		481,728

GERMAN NET IMPORTS OF CONCENTRATES.

Crop	1912-13	1922
	1,000 short tons	1,000 short tons
Barley ....:	3,107	267
Oats..........................:	152	85
Maize ....:	935	1,085
Bran etc. ....:	1,462	121
Rice offals ....:	191	69
Total ....:	5,847	1,629

Source: Report from U.S. Agricultural Representative in Berlin, Germany.

ANIMALS SLAUGHTERED UNDER INSPECTION IN GERMANY.

	Year	Steers	Bulls	Cows	Young cattle over 3 months	Calves under three months
Former Territory of 1 9 1 3	1912	524,236	423,086	1,731,996	961,391	4,366,302
	1913	518,244	498,138	1,633,561	879,032	4,088,445
Territory of 1 9 2 1	1913	494,352	471,156	1,491,829	804,192	3,737,957
	1919		629,232	909,655	994,709	892,456
	1920		532,022	895,606	661,855	1,223,735
	1921	366,169	369,992	1,305,539	875,852	3,126,971
Present territory excluding Saar Section:......	1913	492,148	466,091	1,463,656	791,452	3,702,536
	1921	359,483	364,635	1,283,536	866,466	3,108,376
	1922	316,357	323,534	1,442,478	965,767	3,207,789
Slaughtering under Inspection during the first 6 months	1921	127,776	151,883	557,565	314,373	1,449,129
	1922	147,131	158,831	724,157	435,490	1,890,369
Slaughtered weights in pounds a	1908	728	683	529	408	88
	1920			342		68
	1921-22	674	580	461	355	86

a Slaughtered (or dressed) weights of animals are important in making comparisons. The German Meat Office has found average slaughtered weights for 1920 as above, and for a general comparison the same weights can be applied to 1919, although average weights were undoubtedly less for that year.

Source: E.C. Squire, U.S. Agricultural Representative in Berlin, Germany.

ANIMALS SLAUGHTERED UNDER INSPECTION IN GERMANY, CONT'D.

	Year	Hogs	Sheep	Goats	Horses & one hoof animals	Dogs
Former Territory of 1 9 1 3....:	1912	18,217,356	2,269,419	474,534	179,113	8,094
	1913	17,872,028	2,092,989	469,798	163,282	7,356
Territory of 1 9 2 1 ......:	1913	16,587,896	1,968,434	422,856	153,564	7,346
	1919	1,367,927				
	1920	3,011,567				
	1921	6,926,602	2,093,762	320,155	149,695	5,482
Present Territory: excluding Saar Section.....:	1913	16,375,542	1,966,893	419,973	153,039	7,344
	1921	6,824,761	2,032,358	315,387	148,679	5,482
	1922	6,516,735	1,769,406	259,551	240,014	13,595
Slaughtering under Inspection during the first 6 months	1921	2,966,666	576,466	142,585	58,192	
	1922	3,956,993	731,871	155,484	94,676	
Slaughtered a weights in pounds	1908	187	48	35	518	
	1920	165	37	35	518	
	1921-22	183	48	35	525	

a The German Health Office, on October 18, 1922, issued a bulletin giving the
average slaughtered weights of animals for 1921 and 1922 on the basis of
weights during the year from April 1, 1921, to March 31, 1922. The
slaughtered weights for 1908 can be taken as representative of pre-war
years.

Source: E.C. Squire, U.S. Agricultural Representative in Berlin, Germany.

NUMBER OF DAIRY ANIMALS, SHEEP AND HOGS IN GERMANY IN 1912, 1913, 1920, 1921 AND 1922.

December 1	Terri- tory	Total	Cattle :Cows 2 yrs. and older	Milk cows	Sheep
1912 .....:	former	20,182,021 :	10,944,283 :	10,205,185 :	5,803,445
1913 .....:	former	20,994,344 :	11,320,460 :	10,555,000 :	5,520,837
1913 .....:	present	18,475,804 :	9,913,418 :	9,475,000 :	
1920 .....:		16,806,791 :	8,790,163 :	7,922.945 :	6,149,803
1921 .....:		16,790,699 :	9,061,598 :	8,247,061 :	6,676,324
1922 .....:		16,309,474 :	8,970,818 :	8,139,828 :	5,745,613
1922 in comparison to:		:	:	:	
1913 .....:	former	- 4,684,870 :	- 2,349,642 :	- 2,415,172 :	224,776
1913 .....:	present	- 2,166,330 :	- 1,002,600 :	- 1,335,172 :	
1920 .....:		- 497,317 :	179,655 :	216,883 :	- 404,190
1921 .....:		- 481,225 :	- 90,780 :	107,232 :	- 930,711

December	Terri- tory	Goats Total	Milk goats (about 2/3)	Hogs Total	Pigs of less than 8 weeks
1912 .....:	former	3,410,396 :	2,608,874 :	21,923,707 :	
1913 .....:	former	3,548,384 :	2,355,600 :	25,659,140 :	
1913 .....:	present	3,164,250 :	2,109,500 :	22,534,407 :	
1920 .....:		4,458,535 :	2,972,360 :	14,179,163 :	2,624,066
1921 .....:		4,295,548 :	2,863,700 :	15,817,819 :	2,980,071
1922 .....:		4,135,950 :	2,757,300 :	14,682,622 :	2,593,680
1922 in comparison to:				:	
1913 .....:	former	587,566 :	401,700 :	- 10,976,518 :	
1913 .....:	present	971,700 :	647,800 :	- 7,850,785 :	
1920 .....:		- 322,585 :	- 215,060 :	503,459 :	- 30,386
1921 .....:		- 159,598 :	- 106,400 :	- 1,135,197 :	- 386,391

GERMAN TRADE IN MILK, CREAM, AND MILK PRODUCTS.
(Tons of 2,000 Pounds).

Item	Year	Imports	Exports	Net imports or exports		Milk equivalent
Milk	1912	47,429	12,967	Import	34,462	34,462
	1913	36,144	13,724	"	22,420	22,420
	1922	10,573	6,057	"	4,516	4,516
Cream	1912	46,241	50	"	46,191	230,955
	1913	48,914	28	"	48,886	244,430
	1922	14	--	"	14	70
Butter Milk	1912	298	4,483	Export	4,185	(1)
	1913	15	4,738	"	4,723	
	1922	--	--		--	
Milk (Dried and prepared	1912	29	5,128	"	5,099	(2) 25,495
	1913	57	9,101	"	9,044	45,220
	1922	4,647	511	Import	4,136	20,680
Cheese (Solid)	1912	21,494	56	"	21,438	214,380
	1913	26,740	143	"	26,597	265,970
	1922	20,850	176	"	20,674	206,740
Cheese (Soft)	1912	2,145	851	"	1,294	12,940
	1913	2,211	659	"	1,552	15,520
	1922	5,142	942	"	4,200	42,000
Butter	1894	7,716	8,598	Export	882	18,522
	1908	38,029	243	Import	37,786	793,506
	1909	49,350	231	"	49,119	1,031,499
	1910	46,406	198	"	46,208	970,368
	1911	61,839	276	"	61,563	1,292,823
	1912	61,288	243	"	61,045	1,281,945
	1913	59,745	298	"	59,447	1,248,387
	1922	1,179	309	"	870	18,270

(1) Buttermilk a by-product - milk equivalent not expressed.
(2) Equivalent taken as five pounds of milk to one of dried or prepared.
Source: Reports from E. C. Squire, Agricultural Representative in Berlin, Germany.

IMPORTS OF MARGARINE MATERIAL AND TALLOW, 1912 - 1922, INTO GERMANY

Item	1912	1913	1920	1921	1922
	Short tons	Short tons	Short tons	Short tons	Short tons
Lard:					
Total ....:	116,978	118,373	136,038	161,162	72,000
From United States.....L	110,672	111,532	125,790 L		63,153
Cleo:					
Total ....:	27,067	29,132	5,604	3,277	14,319
From United States.....:	22,746	21,641	3,320		11,505
From Argentina ....:	992	1,377	114		
Premier Jus (Oleo Stock):					
Total ....:	21,655	22,401	8,230	6,245	8,347
From United States ....:	12,153	9,480	4,256		3,825
From Argentina.........:	4,918	7,943	837		2,350
Tallow:					
Total ....:	23,621	29,568	15,954	38,657	34,488
From United States ....:	3,441	3,913	4,656		9,254
Cotton Seed Oil:					
Total ....:	29,623	17,945	13,729	26,888	2,935
From United States ....:	22,895	11,022	4,619		410
Fish Oil:					
Total ....:	40,952	55,715	18,631		69,027

Note: Exports of above fats and oils are unimportant.
Source: Report of U.S.Agricultural Representative at Berlin, Germany.

Index.

Historic, archived document

Do not assume content reflects current
scientific knowledge, policies, or practices.

CPSIA information can be obtained
at www.ICGtesting.com
Printed in the USA
BVHW031156021118
531990BV00020B/1578/P